Chicago/Kezys

Chicago/Kezys

64 Photographs of Chicago
By Algimantas Kezys, S.J.

A Campion Book

Loyola University Press
Chicago   60657

Design by Mary Golon

Library of Congress Cataloging in Publication Data

Kezys, Algimantas.
   Chicago/Kezys : 64 photographs of Chicago.
   1. Chicago (Ill.) – Description – 1981-   – Views.
2. Architecture – Illinois – Chicago – Pictorial works.
3. Photography, Artistic.   I. Title.
F548.37.K49   1983   779′.9977311   82-17175
ISBN 0-8294-0408-2

Contents

Marina City, 1967

Foreword

Welcome to Chicago—but of course these pictures really have as much to do with the visual sensitivities of their maker, Algimantas Kezys, as they do with the steel and concrete and people of Chicago. A photographer's "place," after all, is behind the camera, where he is bound to explore and exercise those internal orders that drive him. He responds to a particular physical location without being dependent upon it or controlled by it. And it is a mark of Kezys' sensitivity, as he has explored his own keen vision through the years, that he consistently sees with insight, compassion, and clarity, despite his busy schedule as a book publisher, director of an art gallery, and a Jesuit priest.

In this third volume of his photographs published by Loyola University Press, Kezys shares his vision of Chicago as a collection of individual moments connected by form, by subject, by association. It is also to some degree an exploration of what photojournalists call "the third effect"—the enriching expansion of two images which, viewed together, resonate with overtones or associations neither may have triggered alone. The two images become a single, third entity which can give rise to emotions or connotations undetected in either of the pair viewed separately. Frequently, and equally satisfying, the two pictures combine to enhance or reinforce a visual statement.

Each of the photographs in this volume was created independently as Kezys made frequent short forays into various parts of the city. It was only after many photographs were printed and viewed that the strength of seeing the work in pairs became increasingly apparent. Al Kezys and George Lane made the basic, perceptive selection and pairings from which this volume has evolved.

While the photographs are seen in pairs, the individual images continue to explore major themes which have appeared throughout the photographer's work. One of these is the use of bold, graphic, silhouette strokes of black and white. Another theme is the observation-at-a-distance of individual people as they walk hallway mazes, tread endless stairways, and otherwise navigate streams of stone and steel that seem to overwhelm them in size and gravity. Yet this seems not a vision of individuals oppressed, but rather a contemplation of solitary, resourceful people living in the flow of a complex and confusing society.

Finally and delightfully, Father Kezys has no pretensions about his work. He approaches the world with neither a heavy brow nor a light head, but with eyes open, with intelligence, and with a wish to see and discover. He has no axes to grind, no messages, no designs or aspirations other than a desire to observe and share what he sees with others. And so he does, with precision and economy.

JOHN ALDERSON
Photography critic
Chicago Sun-Times

Lake Shore Drive at Oak Street, 1965

Preface

There was a time when I considered myself a collector of "design pictures." Each photo was independent, complete in its own right, with no story to tell other than that of its own beauty. And by "beauty" I meant the formal aspect of the picture.

Though I accepted that, indeed professed it, I knew at the same time that in my own work I was not practicing the highest kind of photographic art. To my mind, the highest form of photographic art was documentary photography: great content combined with perfect form. For me, though, it existed as an ideal to be admired and enjoyed in other's work, not my own. I consciously chose an inferior type of photographic activity, one that emphasized form without much concern for the content of the picture. I felt that one ought not practice any art except in his own way—and my way was "form over content."

Deep down, however, I knew I wasn't satisfied. How can one be satisfied with himself while admitting that one form of photography is superior to another and then choosing to do the other? So I tried my hand at real documentation on several occasions— and failed dismally. A notable example of this was a commission I accepted during Jimmy Carter's campaign to win the Democratic nomination for President. I was asked to photograph the town Jimmy called his own. I worked two solid weeks documenting every little corner of Plains, Georgia, its people and their activities. I even got a chance to shoot a few pictures of the candidate himself. And the result? More than fifty of my photographs were published in the book, some of them featured in full-page spreads. But the majority of the pictures that were printed were ones I had taken previously and elsewhere. They were picked from my files because the editors thought they symbolically expressed the truth about Jimmy Carter better than the pictures I had actually taken of him and of his town!

I went right back to my "design picture" mentality, more determined than ever not to deviate from this rule again. I even self-published a four-volume set of Posters in which I deliberately picked pictures at random, numbered them from 1 to 128, and divided them in four equal parts to make up the sets. I wanted to stress the idea that each of those photos had to be taken individually—without regard to any other picture in the set—and in total disregard of its content. It was "design" that really mattered, nothing else but design.

And then one day it dawned on me, after much reflection and soul-searching, that the problem was really more conceptual than real. To put it bluntly, "it was all in my mind." There was nothing wrong with my pictures—just with my attitude toward those pictures. The photographs I had been producing over the years were, after all, documentary in nature. They weren't contrived, or pre-visualized, or manufactured in the darkroom. They were simply shots of the real world in which we live. I had taken most of them on summer travels, shooting whatever came my way—nature, people, cities, events—in a photo-journalistic fashion. Even though I was searching in them for "form," I was engaged at the same time in recording something real. In themselves, they were never anything else but "documentary."

It is a relief, finally, to be able to say this. There is a sense of peace, as well as accomplishment, in the feeling of having arrived at a long-desired goal.

To make a long story short, in this volume of photographs I am presenting my pictures in a new way; namely, as documentation of a place, the city of Chicago. The pictures here are not to be taken singly, out of context, or merely admired for their design value. They are meant to tell a story; they are my impressions of a real place, the city of Chicago, where I have lived and worked for the last twenty years of my life.

ALGIMANTAS KEZYS

Sears Tower, 1979

1/The Art of Architecture

First National Bank of Chicago, 1981

John Hancock Building, 1970

Time-Life Building, 1970

Pablo Picasso sculpture, Richard J. Daley Plaza, 1967

Alexander Calder stabile, Federal Center Plaza, 1982

Traffic signal, State and Madison Streets, 1982

Clock on Palmer House, State and Monroe Streets, 1982

Continental Illinois National Bank, 1967

Stairway to Ogden Avenue, near Division and Halsted Streets, 1966

Xerox Building, 55 West Monroe Street, 1981

Kinzie Steak House and Marina City, 1979

Lake Point Tower, 1968

Lake Point Tower and William King sculpture, Art 1982 Chicago

Oak Street pedestrian underpass at Lake Shore Drive, 1982

Peep Shows, Old Town, 1982

Northern Trust Banking Center, 120 East Oak Street, 1982

Lobby, Stone Container Building, 360 North Michigan Avenue, 1982

The Rookery, 209 South LaSalle Street, 1967

Stairway, Michigan Avenue, 1965

2/Parks, Plazas, and Public Places

The Art Institute of Chicago, Columbus Drive facade, 1982

Pioneer Court, North Michigan Avenue, 1982

Navy Pier Auditorium, Art 1982 Chicago

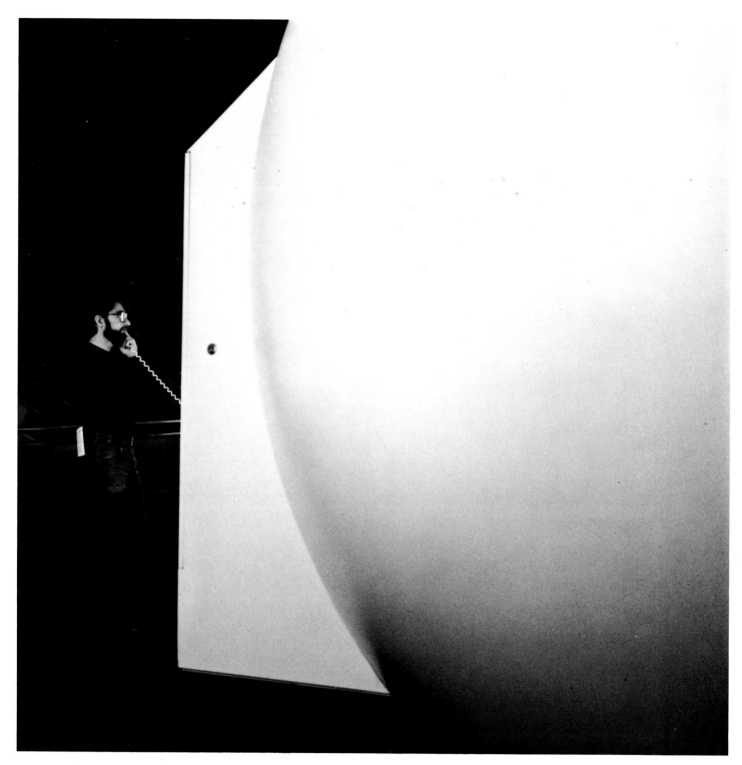

Museum of Science and Industry, 1980

John G. Shedd Aquarium, 1967

Newberry Library, 1982

Chicago Public Library Cultural Center, 1981

Chicago Public Library Cultural Center, 1981

C. D. Peacock, State and Monroe Streets, 1981

Lincoln Park Zoo, 1967

Lincoln Park Zoo, 1967

Totem pole, Lincoln Park at Addison Street, 1982

Boat at Belmont Harbor, 1982

Museum of Science and Industry, Viking exhibit, 1982

Dinghy at Belmont Harbor, 1982

Replica of Viking ship, Lincoln Park Zoo, 1982

Wieboldt's, northwest corner Madison and Wabash, 1981

3/Urban Observations

Hyatt Regency Chicago, 1982

Chicago River at Michigan Avenue, 1966

Chicago River at Michigan Avenue, 1966

Hyatt Regency Chicago, 1982

State Street Mall, 1982

Carson Pirie Scott & Co., State Street Store, 1982

Carson Pirie Scott & Co., State Street Mall, 1982

Palmer House, 1982

View from Doral Plaza Building, 1982

Carson Pirie Scott & Co., State Street Window, 1982

Carson Pirie Scott & Co., State Street Window, 1982

Marshall Field & Co., State Street Store, 1981

Marshall Field & Co., State Street Store, 1981

Carson Pirie Scott & Co., 1981

Water Tower Place, 1981

CBS Studios, 1982

Northwestern University, Chicago Campus, June, 1982

Chicago Sun-Times Building, 1982

Michigan Avenue, 1982

Field Museum of Natural History, 1982

The Art Institute of Chicago, 1981

University of Illinois, Chicago Circle Campus, 1981

University of Illinois, Chicago Circle Campus, 1981

John Henry sculpture, One Illinois Center, 1982

Behind Holy Family Church, Roosevelt Road at May Street, 1970

Editor's Note

Algimantas Kezys is a photographer who sees the familiar in an unfamiliar way. He sees the same things that we happen to see, but he sees them in a unique, exciting way with his camera. "I know that my 'moment of glory' " wrote Kezys, "is the moment of seeing and discovering." Through his photographs, his vision enlarges our vision. With his help we can begin to see the world around us in a new way.

Al Kezys was born in Lithuania in 1928. He came to the United States in 1950 and in that same year joined the Society of Jesus. He was ordained a Jesuit priest in 1961 and soon afterwards came to live and work in Chicago. Kezys has had many exhibitions of his work in many cities across the United States, in Europe, and in Canada. His photos have appeared in many books, magazines, and newspapers. Loyola University Press has published several books of his photography, the first, *photographs/Algimantas Kezys, S.J.*, was based upon an exhibit of his work at The Art Institute of Chicago. This volume, however, is the first collection of his photographs in which all the pictures were taken in one place, in Chicago. It is a special kind of documentary, the city of Chicago as seen by Algimantas Kezys.

Most of the pictures which appear in a square format in this book and those which appear without "frames" were taken with a Rolleiflex or a Hasselblad camera. Those pictures in rectangular formats that are printed with "frames" were taken with a Leicaflex or a Nikon F camera. Some of the pictures were taken with a 90 mm lens, others with a 50 mm lens, and still others with a 20 mm wide angle lens. All of the pictures were developed, enlarged, and printed by Kezys himself. In no instance were two negatives superimposed, nor were any other alterations other than cropping made in the darkroom. Each print was made from one negative.

Loyola University Press is pleased to present this volume of photographs by Algimantas Kezys in the hope that it will be a delight to the people of Chicago, a special souvenir for visitors, and a unique presentation of our city to our friends in other places.

GEORGE A. LANE, S.J.
Editor

About this book

Chicago/Kezys was designed by Mary Golon. It was set by Lakeshore Typographers, Inc. The text is 11 on 13 Optima; the photo captions are 10 point in the same face. It was printed by Photopress, Inc., on Warren's 100-pound Lustro Offset Enamel Dull and was bound by Zonne Bookbinders.